FROM SEA to SHINING SEA

MASSACHUSETTS

JOAN LEOTTA

Consultants

MELISSA N. MATUSEVICH, PH.D.

Curriculum and Instruction Specialist
Blacksburg, Virginia

SUSAN NICHOLS

Library Media Specialist

Douglas Elementary School
Douglas, Massachusetts

CHILDREN'S PRESS®

A DIVISION OF SCHOLASTIC INC.

New York • Toronto • London • Auckland • Sydney • Mexico City
New Delhi • Hong Kong • Danbury, Connecticut

Massachusetts is located in the region called New England. Other states in this region are Connecticut, Maine, New Hampshire, Rhode Island, and Vermont.

Project Editor: Lewis K. Parker
Art Director: Marie O'Neill
Photo Researcher: Marybeth Kavanagh
Design: Robin West, Ox and Company, Inc.
Page 6 map and recipe art: Susan Hunt Yule
All other maps: XNR Productions, Inc.

Library of Congress Cataloging-in-Publication Data
Leotta, Joan
    Massachusetts / by Joan Leotta.
      p. cm—(From sea to shining sea)
    Includes bibliographical references (p.) and index.
    ISBN 0-516-22486-7
1. Massachusetts—Juvenile literature. [1. Massachusetts.] I. Title. II. From sea to shining sea (Series)

F64.3 .L46 2001
974—dc21   00-069384

TABLE of CONTENTS

CHAPTER ONE

INTRODUCING THE BAY STATE

Boston Common is a public garden where people often ride the swan boats.

In **1620 a group of English people called Pilgrims** first stepped on the shores of what we call Massachusetts near Boston. They built their homes in a protected bay area near present-day Boston and called their settlement the Bay Colony. Later, James II, the king of England, named the area the "Massachusetts Bay Colony" after the Massachuset Native American tribe. In the language of that tribe, Massachusetts means "small hill" or "place near the great hill." Today, the state's nickname is the Bay State.

Massachusetts was one of the thirteen original colonies of the United States. The people of Massachusetts have played major roles throughout American history. They have also contributed to greatness in areas such as music, literature, science, and sports since the time of the first settlers.

What comes to mind when you think of Massachusetts?

- The Mayflower docking at Plymouth and the Pilgrims arriving
- Minutemen fighting the British
- Sturbridge Village and a step back to the 1830s
- People skiing in the Berkshire Mountains
- Mills using water power at Lowell
- Colonial churches throughout the state
- Musicians playing at Tanglewood
- President John F. Kennedy serving his country
- Witches at Salem
- Fishermen catching lobsters off the coast

The state is forty-fifth in land size compared to the other states and thirteenth in the number of people. Despite its small size, there's plenty to see and do in the Bay State. Read on to sample the history, people, places, and fun of Massachusetts.

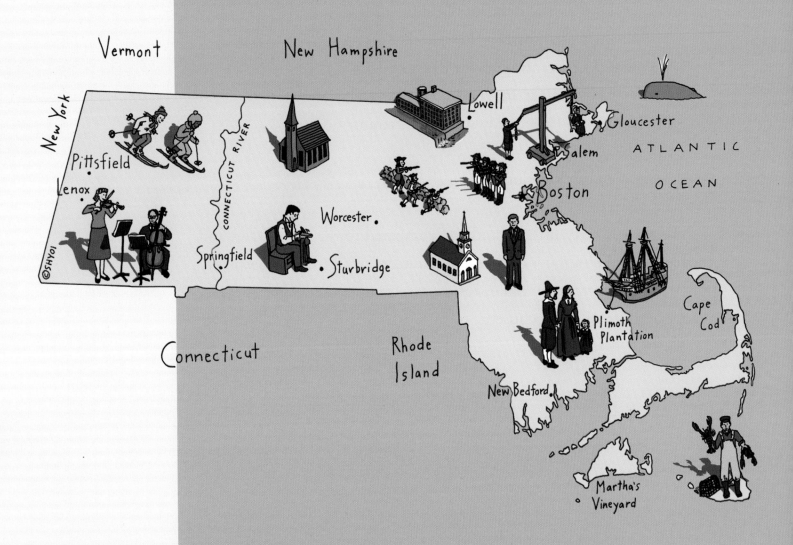

Vermont

New Hampshire

New York

Connecticut

Rhode
Island

New York

Pittsfield

Lenox

CONNECTICUT RIVER

Springfield

Worcester

Sturbridge

Lowell

Gloucester

Salem

Boston

ATLANTIC

OCEAN

Plimoth
Plantation

Cape
Cod

New Bedford

Martha's
Vineyard

CHAPTER TWO

THE LAND OF MASSACHUSETTS

Massachusetts is easy to find on a map of the United States. Look in the northeast corner for the hook-shaped peninsula that extends into the Atlantic Ocean. Besides the land of Massachusetts, two island groups and two islands are also part of the state—the Boston Harbor Islands, Elizabeth Islands, Nantucket, and Martha's Vineyard. There are 22 small islands in the Elizabeth Islands, and about 30 in the Boston Harbor Islands.

In the United States, Massachusetts is the sixth smallest state. Massachusetts covers 9,241 square miles (23,934 square kilometers). It stretches 190 miles (306 km) from east to west and 110 miles (177 km) north to south at its widest points. At one time, Maine was a part of Massachusetts until Maine became a separate state in 1820.

Colorful sugar maples and ash present an autumn scene near Williamstown.

FIND OUT MORE

A peninsula is a land formation that has water on three sides. Can you find other peninsulas on a map of the United States?

FIND OUT MORE

How large was Massachusetts before Maine became a separate state? Was Massachusetts the largest state in the United States before 1820?

BORDERS

On Massachusetts' northern border lie New Hampshire and Vermont. The southern border of the state touches Connecticut and Rhode Island. New York is to the west of Massachusetts and the Atlantic Ocean forms the state's eastern border. Massachusetts enjoys a shoreline of 192 miles (309 km), if you measure the coast with a straight line. If you count each little cove and inlet on Cape Cod, the shoreline measures about 1,980 miles (3,187 km)!

If you were to start in the east and drive across the state to the west, you would travel through four different types of land. Your journey would take you across beaches, over rolling hills, through river valleys, and into mountains.

REGIONS

Coastal Lowland

This region makes up the eastern third of Massachusetts. It includes the Cape Cod peninsula and the islands, and extends forty miles inland from the coast. On the edges of these lowlands, ocean waves lap the sand and rocks. The Massachusetts coastline offers many good natural harbors, especially around Boston, which is a major U.S. port. Except for the Cape Cod dunes, mountains of sand formed by wind, and a few small, rounded hills near Boston, most of the lowlands are flat.

The salt marshes of the coastal lowland are home to gulls, ducks, terns, and other shore birds. Cranberries grow well in the watery, sandy bogs of southeastern Massachusetts. From the tops of those great sand dunes near the town of Provincetown on Cape Cod you might even see whales playing in the water.

Grasses sprout out of the sandy dunes of Cape Cod National Seashore.

Eastern New England Upland

This area extends forty to sixty miles (64–97 km) wide from the end of the Coastal Lowland to the west. It includes many sloping hills and streams. The land slopes down toward the Connecticut Valley lowland.

This area has monadnocks, isolated hills or mountains of hard rock that resisted erosion. Wachusett Mountain, the area's highest point, is a monadnock. Skiers and hikers enjoy the mountain's many trails and beautiful views.

Connecticut Valley Lowland

This thin, sausage-shaped area is in the center of the state. The Connecticut River is the most important geographic feature of this section. It is also the longest river in Massachusetts—sixty-six miles (106 km) long. This area offers rich soil for farming.

Many streams empty into the Connecticut River. Cottonwood and silver maple shade those streams, which are often full of salmon, sturgeon, and shad. This part of the state is a great place for any river water sport and fishing. Thousands of years ago the soft soil of this area was imprinted with the footprints and bones of many dinosaurs. This is the part of the state to visit if you are looking for dinosaur tracks!

Western New England Upland

The Upland includes the Berkshire Valley, a ten-mile-wide (16 km) strip of land that runs almost the entire length of the state. Dairy farmers find this an excellent place for cows to graze. The Berkshire Hills lead up to the Green Mountains.

The Green Mountain range extends down from Vermont into Massachusetts. The state flower, the Mayflower, grows here. Mount Greylock, a mountain in this range, is the highest point in the state at 3,491 feet (1,064 m).

FIND OUT MORE

What is the highest point in the United States? Is that point higher or lower than Mount Greylock?

This is a view from the state's highest point, Mount Greylock.

On a six-mile-wide (10 km) section of land in the very northwestern tip of the state are the Taconic Mountains. One of the Taconic's highest mountains in Massachusetts, Mount Everett, is 2,602 feet (793 m). It is the second-highest mountain in the state.

RIVERS, LAKES, AND PONDS

Massachusetts has many natural water resources. There are many rivers, streams and lakes. The state's longest river, the Connecticut River, runs southward down the middle of the state. The Housatonic, another important river, is in southwestern Massachusetts. In the past, it supplied power for the area's early industries.

The Merrimack River flows down into the state from New Hampshire in the northeast. After it enters Massachusetts, the Merrimack changes course and flows into the Atlantic Ocean. The Blackstone River, located in south-central Massachusetts, flows from Worcester into Rhode Island. It is an important natural and cultural resource to the state.

The Charles, Mystic, and Neponset Rivers are important rivers in the eastern half of the state. They flow into Boston Bay. The Charles River runs right through the city of Boston, separating the town of Cambridge from Boston.

Massachusetts has more than one thousand lakes and ponds. The largest is an artificial lake, Quabbin Reservoir (39 square miles or 101 sq km). The largest natural lake is Assawompset Pond.

EXTRA! EXTRA!

If all of the rivers in the state were put together they would stretch 4,230 miles (6,808 km)!

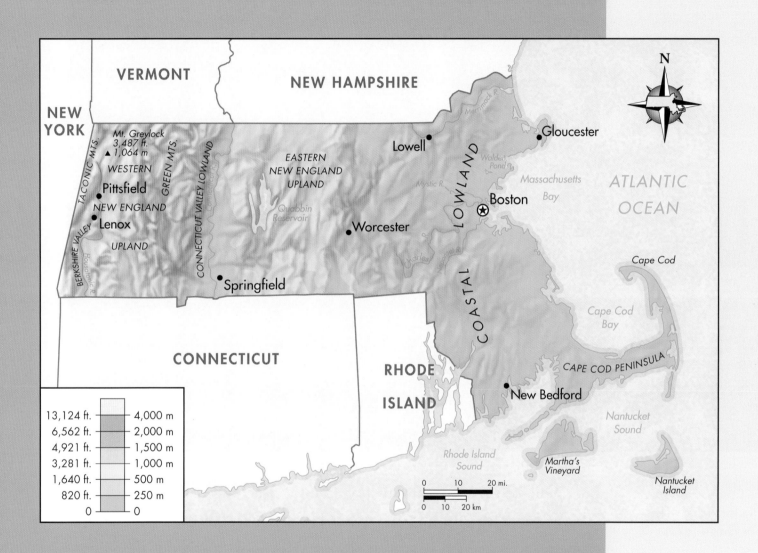

VERMONT

NEW HAMPSHIRE

NEW YORK

Mt. Greylock
3,487 ft.
▲ 1,064 m

WESTERN

TACONIC MTS.

GREEN MTS.

Pittsfield

NEW ENGLAND

Lenox

UPLAND

BERKSHIRE VALLEY

Housatonic R.

CONNECTICUT VALLEY LOWLAND

Connecticut R.

EASTERN
NEW ENGLAND
UPLAND

Quabbin
Reservoir

Lowell

Merrimack R.

Walden
Pond

Mystic R.

Boston

Gloucester

Massachusetts
Bay

ATLANTIC
OCEAN

Worcester

Charles R.

Blackstone R.

Springfield

CONNECTICUT

RHODE

ISLAND

COASTAL LOWLAND

Cape Cod

Cape Cod
Bay

CAPE COD PENINSULA

New Bedford

Nantucket
Sound

Rhode Island
Sound

Martha's
Vineyard

Nantucket
Island

N

13,124 ft.	4,000 m
6,562 ft.	2,000 m
4,921 ft.	1,500 m
3,281 ft.	1,000 m
1,640 ft.	500 m
820 ft.	250 m
0	0

0   10   20 mi.

0   10   20 km

13

The Connecticut River flows through a valley near Turners Falls.

One of the most famous ponds in Massachusetts is Walden Pond, near Concord. In the 1840s, writer Henry David Thoreau built a cabin there and wrote a book called *Walden*. His book tells about the importance of each person's relationship to the wilderness. Over the years those writings have inspired many people to work toward preserving the environment.

Massachusetts has four distinct seasons. The climate in the eastern part of the state is influenced by the Atlantic Ocean and the warm air currents that flow over its waters. This makes the temperatures on the eastern side of the state generally milder—cooler in the summer and warmer in the winter.

The differences in temperature caused by being near the ocean can be seen in the variation of the temperatures between Boston in the east and the city of Pittsfield in the west. In Boston the average January temperature is 29°F (–2°C). Boston's July average temperature is 72° F (22°C). Pittsfield, in the western part of the state, averages 21° F (–6°C) in January and only reaches highs of 68° to 70°F (20°C to 21°C) in July.

Both rain and snow together (precipitation) average about 42 inches a year across the state. More snow falls in the western part of the state, in the mountains. On the coast, sometimes violent hurricanes (powerful tropical storms) bring heavy rains. Some of the worst hurricane damage of the last century occurred in 1938, 1985, and 1991.

One storm that struck in 1938 was so powerful that it was called the "Long Island Express." The storm hit land in Long Island, New York and roared up the New England coast like a freight train, at a rate of 70 miles per hour, the fastest record ever for a hurricane. This hurricane killed more

FIND OUT MORE

Precipitation is water that falls from the sky. It can come as snow, rain, sleet, and even hail or ice. What is the average total precipitation in your area? How does that compare to the average in Massachusetts?

than six hundred people and destroyed about 8,000 homes and 3,000 boats.

Other hurricanes have also caused great damage. Hurricane Gloria in 1985 caused about $900 million dollars in damage. In 1991 Hurricane Bob caused $1.5 billion in damage. Six out of every ten homes in the northeast section of Massachusetts lost electric power during this storm. Another hurricane later that year had little effect on land, but wreaked havoc in the Atlantic Ocean. In October 1991 the U.S. Coast Guard flew into the thick of the storm off the coast of Massachusetts to rescue a fishing boat and its crew. The story of that rescue was written into a book and later made into a movie called *The Perfect Storm.*

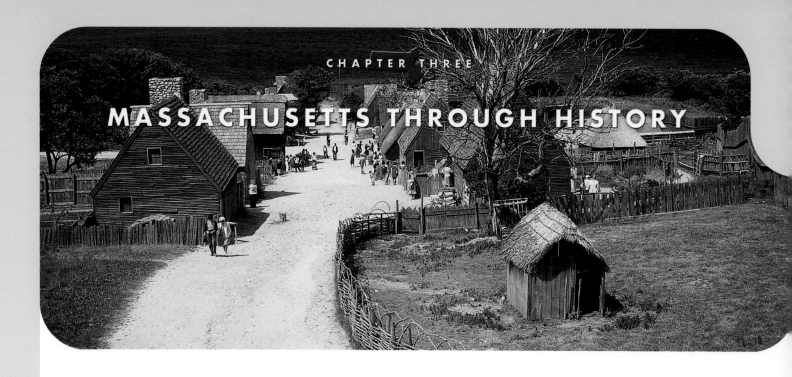

CHAPTER THREE

MASSACHUSETTS THROUGH HISTORY

Native Americans probably came to what is now called Massachusetts about 3,000 years ago. These tribes included the Wampanoag in the southeast; the Massachuset in the northeast; the Nauset on Cape Cod; the Nipmuc, Pennacook, and Mohegan tribes in the central part of the state; and the Pocumtuc in the west.

Most of these people lived in permanent villages. Their round homes had a hole in the center to let out the smoke from the indoor fires. The Wampanoag tribe called their round homes *wettus*. Large family groups lived in long, rectangular homes called *longhouses* of bark and wood.

Women built the houses and wove reed mats used to decorate the inner walls and keep the homes warm in winter. They also made pottery and used finger weaving to make fishing nets and net-like storage bags to hang in their homes. The women used stone hoes and grew corn, beans, and pumpkins, among other crops, in the gardens.

Plimoth Plantation at Plymouth is a re-creation of the Pilgrims's settlement.

At Plimoth Plantation, an interpreter shows how the Wampanoags made a canoe.

Men made canoes from logs called dugout canoes, fished with nets, and hunted with bows and arrows. Some of the tribes on the coast hunted whales with long spears. The chief and sachem, or medicine man, were tribal leaders.

Many early Europeans who came to visit traded with the Algonquians. When the Algonquians traded with or worked for the visitors, they often learned their language. Native Americans who could speak English were very helpful to later settlers.

Who were the first Europeans to set foot in what is now Massachusetts? It might have been Leif Ericson of Iceland. There is evidence that he and his crew of Norsemen visited North America around A.D. 1,000. He may have sailed past the coast of Massachusetts. In 1497, an Italian explorer named Giovanni Caboto—called John Cabot by the Englishmen who paid for his voyage—sailed along the coast of New England.

Records of shipwrecks and crew names lead historians to think that Miguel Cortereal, a Portuguese explorer, may have lived with the Native Americans after he wrecked his boat off the coast of Massachusetts in the early 1500s. He also left an inscription carved in stone to record his stay. Dighton Rock in Fall River bears these words: *M. Cortereal 1511 by God's grace the leader of the Native Americans.* Today, you can see the rock and its carvings at Dighton Rock State Park.

In 1602 English explorer Bartholomew Gosnold named Cape Cod for the many codfish he found in the waters there. He also named the island of Martha's Vineyard after his daughter, Martha, and for the many grapevines on the island. In 1607 the French explorer, Samuel de Champlain, sailed up and down the coast and made maps of the entire area as far as Canada. But these sailors and explorers did not come with their families and they made no attempt to settle down there.

EXTRA! EXTRA!

Plimoth Plantation in Plymouth recreates the Pilgrims' first seventeenth-century English settlement and their ship, the *Mayflower.* Just outside the fence of the village, as it was in the 1600s, lies the home of Hobbamock, a Wampanoag who left his village and lived nearby. In 1623, Pilgrim Edward Altham wrote of him: "Only without our pale (the fence) dwells Hobbamock, his wives and his family, (he) who is our friend and our interpreter."

The Pilgrims were the first Europeans who came with their families to make Massachusetts their new homeland. The Pilgrims were a group of English "separatists." This meant that they were separate in their religious beliefs from the Church of England, which was the official church of the country. King James said these people could not stay in England and worship God as they wished, so they asked King James if they could live in the Americas instead. The King agreed to allow them to form a colony.

On September 6, 1620, 102 passengers left England on the *Mayflower*. Less than half of the people onboard were Separatists. The ship was not large—it was 100 feet long (30 m) and about thirty feet wide (10 m). Among the Separatist families were the Brewsters, Bradfords, Allertons, Fullers, Hopkins, Mullins, and Turners.

The crossing from England to Massachusetts took sixty-five days. The trip across the Atlantic Ocean was not easy. There were storms on the seas and arguments on the ship. Some people wanted to turn back. The Pilgrims, called "saints" by their leader, William Bradford, did not always get along with the explorers and soldiers, whom he called "strangers." It was Bradford who first called the Separatists "Pilgrims."

The Pilgrims planned to sail to Virginia to live near the other English settlers in Jamestown (settled in 1607) but a series of winter storms forced them to land early. On December 11, 1620, the *Mayflower* landed at what is now called Plymouth. They carved the year into a large rock. William Bradford described the landing, "Being thus passed the

vast ocean and a sea of troubles—no friends to welcome us . . . or inns . . . no houses or towns. And for now it was Winter, subject to cruel and violent storms . . . dangerous to travel to known places, much more to an unknown coast."

Before the group left their ship to build homes, the men wrote a set

This illustration shows the Pilgrims first touching land in the New World.

of rules to help them live together. It was called the "Mayflower Compact." It is the first set of written laws to govern people in the New World. An important principle of the Compact, still used in our government today, is the idea that the opinion of the majority will be law. The Mayflower Compact was the first document to provide self-government in the Americas.

Upon first meeting, both the Pilgrims and the Wampanoags offered gifts.

Soon after their arrival, the Pilgrims met several Native Americans. First they met Samoset, a Wampanoag sachem who spoke English. Later, he brought Massasoit, a Wampanoag chief, and another Indian named Squanto or Tisquantum. Squanto was a member of the Patuxet tribe. His tribe had once lived in Plymouth, in the same place the Pilgrims had settled. When Squanto was young, he had been kidnapped and taken to Spain as a slave. He escaped to England and it was there that he learned to speak English. He eventually found his way back home, only to discover that sickness had killed his entire tribe. Massasoit's tribe let Squanto live with them.

On March 22, 1621, Massasoit signed a treaty with the Pilgrims. The treaty lasted more than fifty years. Later, when the Pequots fought the colonists (1635–1636), Massasoit and his tribe honored their agreement not to fight against the Pilgrims.

In the fall of 1621, the Pilgrims decided to have a festival to celebrate God's help in keeping the colony alive. They invited Massasoit to the celebration. This "Thanksgiving Festival" was a part of a long tradition of harvest thanksgiving festivals that were held in Europe. This was one of the first such celebrations held in the New World.

WHO'S WHO IN MASSACHUSETTS?

William Bradford (1590–1657) was the leader of the Pilgrim colony. Each year for thirty years he was elected the governor of the colony.

EXTRA! EXTRA!

John Alden was a Pilgrim who later became governor of the colony. He married another Pilgrim named Priscilla Mullins. A nineteenth-century Massachusetts poet, Henry W. Longfellow, wrote a poem, "The Courtship of Miles Standish." The poem says that John was too shy to speak to Priscilla so he had Miles Standish, an English soldier, speak for him. Priscilla is said to have answered: "Speak for yourself, John!"

Chief Massasoit offers the peace pipe to the Pilgrims.

MASSACHUSETTS BAY COLONY

In 1628 a large group of Puritans arrived from England. The group was led by Reverend John White, who had formed the New England Company to build other settlements near the Plymouth Colony. They settled an area they called Cape Ann. Another settlement also began in 1628 in Naumkeag, known today as Salem. In 1630 these settlements combined to form the Massachusetts Bay Colony. John Winthrop was appointed the first governor of the colony, which included Mishawum (now Charlestown), Shawmut (now Boston), Roxbury, Watertown, and Dorchester.

Within ten years, the Massachusetts Bay Colony had more than 16,000 people living within twenty towns. Other groups of colonists established settlements farther inland, such as Springfield to the west. The Puritans wanted to expand their colony and they did so by taking land from local Native American tribes. Various tribes were angered at having their land taken. They fought back and attacked the colonists. To resist the

EXTRA! EXTRA!

The menu for the three-day celebration of Thanksgiving included corn, squash, and beans. They may have had wild turkey and other birds and they certainly had venison (deer meat). Pilgrim children helped prepare the feast. They gathered wood for the fire, and helped prepare the vegetables and the meat.

attacks, the Massachusetts Bay Colony, Connecticut, New Haven, and Plymouth formed the Confederation of New England in 1643.

This was not a good time for the Pilgrims. Chief Massasoit had been a close friend and peacemaker. When he died, his son Metacom, also known as "Philip," became the chief. Over time, tension arose between the Natives and the English as they each placed unreasonable demands on each other. Eventually, Metacom led his warriors against the colonists. A series of battles came to be known as King Philip's War (1675–1676) during which about one thousand people were killed. Metacom himself was killed, and the Natives were defeated. Afterward, many natives left the area while others were used as servants.

In 1691 Plymouth Colony joined with the Massachusetts Bay Colony. The new group was called the Province of Massachusetts. The king of England appointed a governor to rule over the province. However, the colony could set its own taxes in order to pay the governor.

At this time in Europe, members of various religious groups believed that witches existed. The Puritans brought these beliefs with them to America. They thought that their problems were caused by witches working with the devil. Out of fear, the Puritans were quick to identify people as witches and tried to destroy them. Many Puritans believed that the Native Americans were controlled by the devil.

The fear of witches led to witchcraft trials in Salem in 1692. The problems began when three young Puritan girls claimed that a slave woman, Tituba, made them sick through witchcraft. Tituba had been born in the West Indies, a group of islands in the Caribbean. The girls

During King Philip's War, the Wampanoags attacked Brookfield.

and their families blamed her for their sickness. The girls also began accusing others in the town of being witches, particularly anyone they didn't like.

Many people began to accuse others—more than one hundred people in all. Trials were held in Salem and other nearby towns

These girls point to a victim whom they accuse of being a witch.

to decide if the charges were true. Nineteen people were put to death, often on such slim evidence as the word of one other person. Governor Phips, the Royal Governor of the Colony, eventually stopped the witch hunters after his own wife was accused.

WHO'S WHO IN MASSACHUSETTS?

Phillis Wheatley (1753–1784) was a slave who was taught to read and write. Born in Africa, she was kidnapped and taken as a slave to Boston, where John and Susannah Wheatley purchased her to be their servant. At age thirteen she began to write poetry and in 1773 Phillis was given her freedom. A book of her poems was published that year. She was the first published American poet of African ancestry.

GROWTH AND REVOLUTION

By 1700 about 100,000 people lived in Massachusetts. Around 1750, people from other European nations began to arrive. For example, Portuguese settlers made their homes on Cape Cod. Many of these people had been fishermen in their homeland and they fished here. Some became whale hunters.

By 1765, the number of people living in Massachusetts had increased to 250,000. Most people lived in Boston and nearby towns. Many had small farms. The rocky soil and cold weather in Massachusetts made farming difficult. The sea was a good source of living for many, either through fishing or trade.

During this time, England and France were fighting battles in Europe. In order to pay for this war, England taxed the colonists. The Sugar Act of 1764 taxed, or charged extra money for, cloth goods, coffee, indigo, wine, and sugar. The English government passed another law in 1765 that allowed English soldiers to live in the homes of colonists. Then, a Stamp Act put a tax on anything that was printed,

In 1765 colonists resisted the Stamp Act by burning the stamps.

EXTRA! EXTRA!

Many men began to form groups called Minutemen. They would be ready "in a minute" to drop their regular jobs of farmer, merchant, or blacksmith and become soldiers to fight the English. They began calling themselves "Patriots." Americans who did not support the idea of revolution were known as "Tories."

such as newspapers, playing cards, and advertisements. In 1767, still another group of laws put taxes on window glass, paint, and tea.

On March 5, 1770 some colonists protested against the taxes at the Customs House in Boston. The colonists threw stones and snowballs at English soldiers. The soldiers fired their guns back at the crowd. Colonists Samuel Gray, Samuel Maverick, James Caldwell, and Crispus Attucks, a former slave, were killed. This event is called the Boston Massacre.

In 1773 England passed the Tea Act. This act actually removed taxes on imported tea, but it put American tea merchants out of business because they couldn't compete with the lower prices of British tea. Colonists felt that the Act was unfair. One of the colonists, Samuel Adams, organized the Boston Tea Party as a protest. Several English ships loaded with tea from the East India Company were sitting in Boston Harbor. The colonists were so angry that they refused to let the ship unload its cargo. Disguised as Native Americans, they dumped tea into the water. This event

angered England. In 1774 the English closed down the port of Boston to all shipping, cutting off an important source of supplies for the area. The colonists grew more resentful of English control with every passing day.

A large amount of ammunition was kept in storage at Lexington and Concord. English troops were sent from Boston to Lexington and Concord to take the ammunition. On April 18, 1775, Paul Revere, William Dawes, and Dr. Samuel Prescott rode through the night to warn people about the coming English troops. A group of minutemen was waiting for the English as they approached Lexington, and shots were fired,

WHO'S WHO IN MASSACHUSETTS?

John Hancock (1737–1793) was a merchant. He was the first person to sign the Declaration of Independence and was the first governor of the state of Massachusetts. Today, putting your signature on paper is known as signing your "John Hancock."

WHO'S WHO IN MASSACHUSETTS?

Abigail Adams (1744–1818) was born in Weymouth. She opposed slavery and was a strong supporter of rights for women. She married John Adams, and is the only First Lady from Massachusetts.

killing several Americans. The British continued on their way to Concord, where another small battle was fought. Over 200 people died in these battles, which started the American Revolution (1775–1783). It was said that the first bullet fired in the war was the "shot heard 'round the world." The Revolutionary War started in Massachusetts, but it soon spread throughout the colonies. In 1776, the English left Boston, ending the fighting in Massachusetts. However, the war continued on until 1783, when the colonies finally gained independence from England.

Massachusetts became a commonwealth in 1780. It adopted its own constitution, or basic laws that run a government. The constitution included a Declaration of Rights. This constitution is the oldest written constitution still used today. It became the basis for the U.S. Constitution and the Bill of Rights (first ten amendments).

On February 6, 1788, Massachusetts became the sixth state of the United States. The following year George Washington was chosen as the first president of the new nation. John Adams of Massachusetts became the vice president.

In 1797, John Adams became the second president of the United States and in 1800 he moved into the newly built White House in Washington, D.C. He was the first president to live in the White House. The house was not quite finished. Mrs. Adams said it was "drafty" and hung her laundry to dry in the East Room, a place that is used to receive guests today.

John Adams was the first vice president of the United States.

A NEW CENTURY

In 1807 the U.S. Government passed the Embargo Act. This law stopped any trade between the United States and foreign countries. Merchants and farmers in Massachusetts were especially hurt by the law. They could not ship any of their products to other countries and they did not have many markets within the United States.

However, times were changing quickly in Massachusetts. The early 1800s brought the Industrial Revolution. In 1814 Francis Cabot Lowell built the first cotton mill in the country that produced finished cloth from raw cotton. His factory was the first in the world to put the machines for spinning yarn and the machines for weaving yarn into cloth in the same buildings. The mill was located in Waltham on the Charles River. Both men and women found jobs in the mill. About two hundred girls and women from nearby farms worked away from home for the first time in their lives. By 1850 the mill produced two million yards of cloth a week.

Many textile mills were built at Lowell where the Merrimack and Concord rivers meet.

Waltham wasn't the only place where industry was starting. In the early 1800s mills cropped up all along the Blackstone River, from Rhode Island to Worcester in Massachusetts. Inside these mills were some of the country's first machines powered by water wheels. The manufacturing revolution began here, and communities developed alongside the mills. Factory work wasn't easy. The work days were long—usually from about five in the morning until seven at night—for six days a week. Workers took a half-hour break for breakfast and an hour for lunch. In many

places, men, women, and children worked in the mills. Some of the children were as young as six years old. Their small fingers were useful to undo tangles that would develop in the yarn in the machinery.

Children worked in the mills with lint-filled air and dangerous machines.

THE CIVIL WAR

As Massachusetts and the northern states developed, life became much different there than it was in the southern states. Factories, mills, and businesses filled the northern states. People were paid wages for their work. Slavery was illegal. In the South, there were some businesses and factories,

WHO'S WHO IN MASSACHUSETTS?

Lucretia Mott (1793–1880) of Nantucket was an anti-slavery and women's rights leader. In 1848 she and another reformer from New York, Elizabeth Cady Stanton, helped organize the movement for women's rights at Seneca Falls, New York. After slavery was abolished, Mott worked for voting rights for African-Americans and then returned to the cause of women's rights, especially the right to vote, called "suffrage."

but most people were farmers. Many farms were small, but cotton, the main crop, was often grown on huge farms called plantations. On plantations, the hard work was done by African-American slaves. Slavery was legal in the South.

When Abraham Lincoln was elected president in 1860, he wanted to put an end to slavery. By this time, slavery had been illegal in Massachusetts for almost eighty years. In protest, the southern states seceded, or left, the Union. They formed their own country called the Confederate States of America. Disagreement between the North and South led to a Civil War (1861–1865). The war started when the Confederates attacked Fort Sumter in South Carolina.

About 150,000 soldiers from Massachusetts joined the Union army in the North. The 54th Massachusetts Volunteer Infantry was the first African-American fighting group in the United States. This regiment was led by Robert Shaw, a white colonel. Sergeant William Carney of the 54th became the first African-American to receive the nation's highest military award, the Medal of Honor. After four years of fighting, the Confederate army surrendered to the Union army in April 1965. Slavery was abolished and the Southern states rejoined the Union. The United States began rebuilding cities and towns that had been destroyed in the war, and the relationship between North and South needed repair, as well. This is known as the Era of Reconstruction.

AFTER THE WAR

After the Civil War, amendments (changes) to the U.S. Constitution provided the rights of citizenship to African-American men. For the first time, they were allowed to vote. However, women were not allowed to vote. Many people who had worked hard for the end of slavery now turned their attention to women's suffrage (the right to vote). Susan B. Anthony and Lucy Stone are two women from Massachusetts who worked hard for women's rights.

THE TWENTIETH CENTURY BEGINS

By 1900 about 2.5 million people lived in Massachusetts. About one out of every three people was an immigrant who had come to the

United States in search of a better life. There were so many people living in Boston that traffic jams had started to occur. In order to ease the traffic, a subway system was built to carry people under Boston Common.

World War I (1914–1918) was called "the Great War" or "the War to End All Wars." It was fought in Europe, and the United States didn't enter the war until 1917. During the war, Massachusetts factories made ships, boots, uniforms, and guns.

When the war ended, factories began to pay lower wages to workers. Prices of many items also went up so that people had a more difficult time buying things they needed. Some companies, such as those that made shoes or clothing, moved to southern states where owners didn't have to pay high wages. Demanding better pay, many workers went on strike, or refused to work. In 1918 there were almost four thousand strikes across the United States.

The Great Depression (1929–1939) caused even more misery for workers. The Great Depression occurred as the stock market crashed in 1929. All over the United States, banks closed. Businesses and factories shut down. In some places half of the workers lost their jobs. Almost immediately, the state of Massachusetts started programs to help people find work. The U.S. government also started several programs, like building roads, parks, and dams, that put many people back to work.

The end of the Great Depression didn't occur until the start of World War II (1939–1945). The war brought business back to Massachusetts' shipyards. Many Bay Staters served in the armed forces and fought bravely. John F. Kennedy rescued some of the crew of his PT boat after it was rammed by a Japanese destroyer. George Bush received the Distinguished Flying Cross for his bravery as a pilot. Both men later became President of the United States.

In 1942, 491 people were killed in the Cocanut Grove Nightclub fire in Boston. When the fire started, the people inside could not open several of the exit doors. Because of that fire, Massachusetts and many other states developed strong fire safety laws.

In the 1950s the citizens of Massachusetts found new ways to earn a living. Companies began to make parts for the country's new efforts to send an American into outer space. The many scientists studying at Massachusetts Institute of Technology and Harvard University were attractive to businesses that worked in science. Boston's Route 128, the country's first highway to "loop" around a city, became known as the "Technology Highway." The power of the Technology Highway grew. The number of scientists working in Massachusetts doubled from 13,000 in 1950 to 26,000 in 1960. MIT in

WHAT'S IN A NAME?

Many names of places in Massachusetts have interesting origins.

Name	Comes from or means
Boston	Boston in Lincolnshire, England, original home of many of the first settlers
Mount Greylock	for Native American Chief Grey Lock
Quabbin	comes from Algonquin language and means "well-watered place"
Martha's Vineyard	Martha, daughter of explorer Bartholomew Gosnold

Lake Webster is also known as Lake Chargoggagoggmanchauggagoggchaubunagungamaugg. This Native American word means, "you fish on your side, I'll fish on mine, and nobody fishes in the middle."

Cambridge continues to be one of the top places in the country for training scientists.

The nation focused on Massachusetts when John Fitzgerald Kennedy of Boston became the first Roman Catholic president in 1961. He was assassinated in 1963. His brother Robert, who had served as attorney general, was assassinated in 1968 when he was trying to run for president. In 1966 Edward Brooke, a Washington, D.C.-born African-American who was living in Massachusetts, became the first African-American elected to the U.S. Senate from Massachusetts.

In the 1960s Boston was the scene of many protests against the Vietnam War. By the end of the Vietnam War the economy of the state began to shift again. Military spending, including shipbuilding, was cut back. The space program was also reduced.

More changes came to Massachusetts in the 1970s and 1980s. In 1974 a Federal Court ordered busing in Boston public schools. Until this time, people went to schools in their own neighborhood. Neighborhoods, however, were not racially mixed. They were still divided on racial and ethnic lines. Now the law required a balance, so buses took children from one neighborhood school to another. The court order was not well accepted and violence erupted. It was not until 1999 that the Boston School Committee ended busing.

In 1980, the state of Massachusetts passed laws against the discrimination of persons with disabilities. National laws against such discrimination were not passed until 1990. The state used much of this decade to improve the environment and eliminate discrimination against its

citizens. In 1988 the Boston Harbor cleanup began. Years of industry had done great damage to the natural resources. Eight years later, the Boston Harbor Islands became a national park.

THE NEW CENTURY

The new millennium began with the Massachusetts Legislature passing strong laws against smoking in public places. It also began with new developments in scientific research. Scientists at MIT announced the creation of a series of intelligent robots that are almost like insects.

Massachusetts continues to attract people looking for opportunities, many of whom come from other countries. The 2000 U. S. Census showed that during the 1990s minority groups in the state gained large numbers. In Boston, Caucasians are in the minority; they make up just under half of Boston's population. Almost a quarter of the population is African-American and fourteen out of one hundred people are Hispanic. In Lawrence, more than half the population is Hispanic. The city with the highest number of Asians is Lowell.

Massachusetts is a leader in high technology and medical research. The state's ability to successfully change directions along with a changing economy is in part due to the hard work and independence of its people.

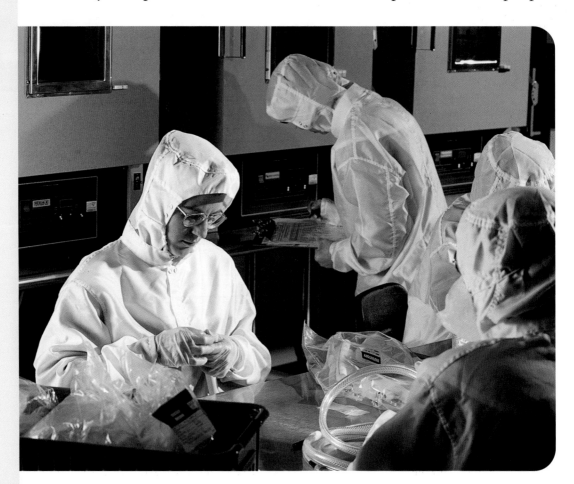

There are many high-technology companies in northeastern Massachusetts.

CHAPTER FOUR

GOVERNING MASSACHUSETTS

A **document that lays out** how people will govern themselves is called a constitution. Massachusetts adopted its first constitution on June 16, 1780. It is the oldest in the United States, adopted before the Revolutionary War ended in 1783. It was in place even before the United States Constitution was created in 1787.

Written by John Adams and John Hancock among others, the Massachusetts constitution divides the state government into three parts, or branches. These are: executive, (administers laws); legislative (makes laws); and judicial (interprets laws). The state constitution sets the age and qualification for voters, too. In Massachusetts, voters must be eighteen years old, a U.S. citizen, and a resident of a city or town.

The writers of the first constitution decided that they would call Massachusetts a "commonwealth." This word comes from the old English word, "commonweal" meaning "the common welfare." Writings of

State government offices are in the State House in Boston.

the founders say that they wanted the older term commonwealth used to highlight the historic role of the people in government. There is no legal difference between the words *state* and *commonwealth*. Kentucky, Pennsylvania, and Virginia are also commonwealths.

The state flag was revised in 1971. The pine tree, which signified the importance of the lumber industry in the state's early years, was taken off the back of the flag design.

THE THREE BRANCHES

Executive Branch

The job of the executive branch is to put laws into action. The governor is the highest elected state official and the head of the executive branch. Governors and the other members of the executive branch are elected for four-year terms. Before the 1960s they served two-year terms. The term was lengthened to four years to give governors more time to put their ideas into action.

A governor's job includes preparing the annual budget, the document that will decide how the state gathers and spends tax money. The governor is also the one who can pardon, or forgive, the jail sentences of prisoners in the state. The governor also appoints people to run the state agencies, and recommends policies and laws, but the legislature must act before they become official. In times of trouble the governor may call upon the state's National Guard, a group of volunteers who are ready to protect and assist the people of Massachusetts.

MASSACHUSETTS GOVERNORS

Name	Term	Name	Term
John Adam Treutlen	1777–1778	Thomas Talbot	1879–1880
John Houstoun	1778–1779	John D. Long	1880–1883
John Wereat	1779–1780	Benjamin F. Butler	1883–1884
George Walton	1779–1780	George D. Robinson	1884–1887
Richard Howley	1780	Oliver Ames	1887–1890
John Hancock	1780–1785	John Q. A. Brackett	1890–1891
James Bowdoin	1785–1787	William E. Russell	1891–1894
John Hancock	1787–1793	Frederick T. Greenhalge	1894–1896
Samuel Adams	1794–1797	Roger Wolcott	1896–1900
Increase Sumner	1797–1799	Winthrop M. Crane	1900–1903
Moses Gill	1799–1800	John L. Bates	1903–1905
Caleb Strong	1800–1807	William L. Douglas	1905–1906
James Sullivan	1807–1808	Curtis Guild, Jr.	1906–1909
Levi Lincoln, Jr.	1808–1809	Eben S. Draper	1909–1911
Christopher Gore	1809–1810	Eugene N. Foss	1911–1914
Elbridge Gerry	1810–1812	David I. Walsh	1914–1916
Caleb Strong	1812–1816	Samuel W. McCall	1916–1919
John Brooks	1816–1823	Calvin Coolidge	1919–1921
William Eustis	1823–1825	Channing H. Cox	1921–1925
Marcus Morton	1825	Alvan T. Fuller	1925–1929
Levi Lincoln	1825–1834	Frank G. Allen	1929–1931
John Davis	1834–1835	Joseph B. Ely	1931–1935
Samuel Armstrong	1835–1836	James M. Curley	1935–1937
Edward Everett	1836–1840	Charles F. Hurley	1937–1939
Marcus Morton	1840–1841	Leverett Saltonstall	1939–1945
John Davis	1841–1843	Maurice J. Tobin	1945–1947
Marcus Morton	1843–1844	Robert F. Bradford	1947–1949
George N. Briggs	1844–1851	Paul A. Dever	1949–1953
George S. Boutwell	1851–1853	Christian A. Herter	1953–1957
John H. Clifford	1853–1854	Foster Furcolo	1957–1961
Emory Washburn	1854–1855	John A. Volpe	1961–1963
Henry J. Gardner	1855–1858	Endicott Peabody	1963–1965
Nathaniel P. Banks	1858–1861	John A. Volpe	1965–1969
John A. Andrew	1861–1866	Francis W. Sargent	1969–1975
Alexander H. Bullock	1866–1869	Michael S. Dukakis	1975–1979
William Claflin	1869–1872	Edward J. King	1979–1983
William B. Washburn	1872–1874	Michael S. Dukakis	1983–1991
Thomas Talbot	1874–1875	William F. Weld	1991–1997
William Gaston	1875–1876	Paul Cellucci	1997–2001
Alexander H. Rice	1876–1879	Jane Swift (acting)	2001–

MASSACHUSETTS STATE GOVERNMENT

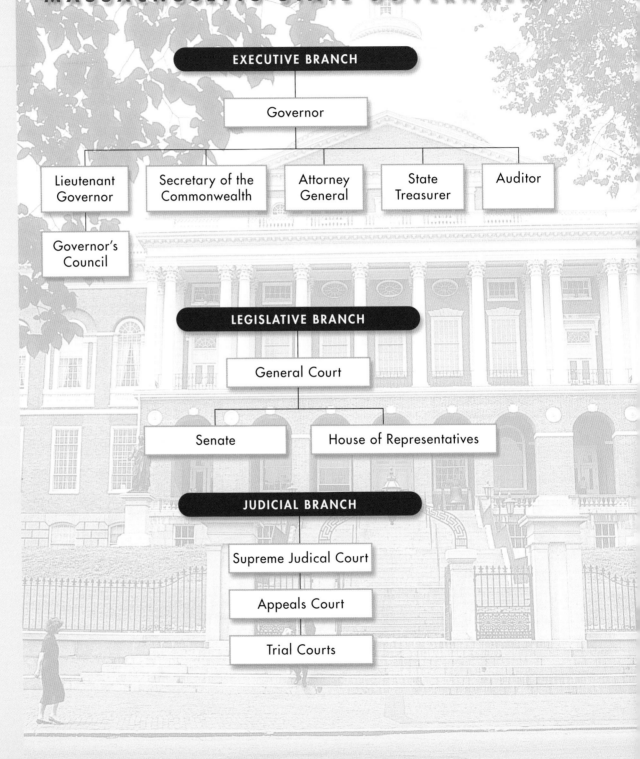

EXECUTIVE BRANCH

Governor

Lieutenant Governor

Secretary of the Commonwealth

Attorney General

State Treasurer

Auditor

Governor's Council

LEGISLATIVE BRANCH

General Court

Senate

House of Representatives

JUDICIAL BRANCH

Supreme Judical Court

Appeals Court

Trial Courts

Legislative Branch

"The Great and General Court" is the official name of the Legislature, as in Puritan times. The legislative branch, which makes new laws, is divided into two parts. These are called "houses" or "chambers." Legislators or members serve either in the House of Representatives or the Senate. Each legislator serves a two-year term. There are 40 members in the State Senate and 160 in the State House. The House and Senate have separate leadership and separate committees to discuss proposed laws (bills).

Judicial Branch

The judicial branch makes sure that the laws are followed. Judges are appointed by the governor. Some are appointed to civil courts (handling cases that are not crimes), and others rule on matters of criminal law. Cases are heard first in civil or criminal court. If either side disagrees with a judge's ruling, the case is sent to an appeals court. If there are still disagreements, the case goes to the state Supreme Judicial Court to review the decision. Supreme Court justices (judges) determine whether the decision made in the lower court was correct. Judges are appointed for life or until they reach age seventy, when the law says they have to retire.

TAKE A TOUR OF BOSTON, THE STATE CAPITAL

Boston is the largest and oldest city in Massachusetts, and one of the oldest in the United States. Boston is also a wonderful place to visit.

Sailboats are a common sight on the Charles River.

A boat trip around Boston Harbor will give you a good look at the city. Then take a walk to see the sights on land. Even though Boston is a large modern city, you can walk to many of its historic points. The city has even painted lines on the ground to help visitors find their way to some of the sights! Probably the most well known "trail" in the city is the Freedom Trail.

The Freedom Trail takes visitors to places that are important in Boston and United States history. It winds though Boston's famous North End, a neighborhood settled by Italian immigrants. The trail also passes many sites that were important in the history of the city's African-Americans and Irish-Americans.

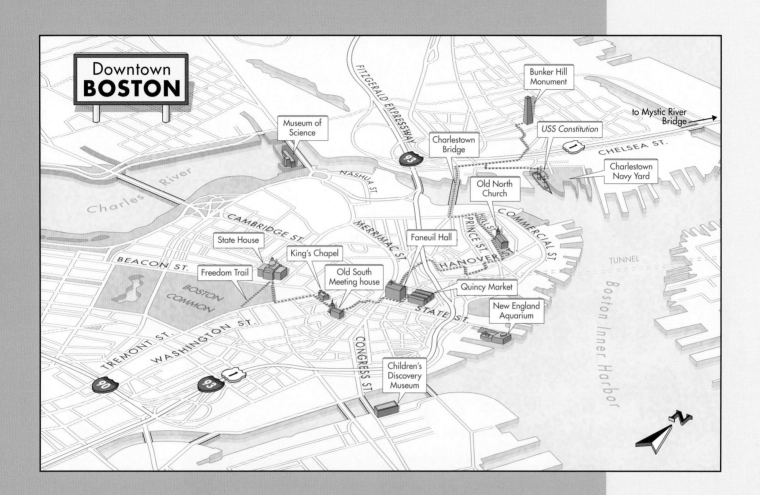

Downtown **BOSTON**

Museum of Science

Bunker Hill Monument

to Mystic River Bridge

Charlestown Bridge

USS Constitution

CHELSEA ST.

Old North Church

Charlestown Navy Yard

FITZGERALD EXPRESSWAY

NASHUA ST.

CAMBRIDGE ST.

State House

MERRIMAC ST.

HANOVER

PRINCE ST.

HULL ST.

COMMERCIAL ST.

King's Chapel

Faneuil Hall

Freedom Trail

BEACON ST.

Old South Meeting house

Quincy Market

TUNNEL

Boston Inner Harbor

BOSTON COMMON

STATE ST.

New England Aquarium

TREMONT ST.

WASHINGTON ST.

CONGRESS ST.

Children's Discovery Museum

Charles River

90

93

N

The Freedom Trail starts at Boston Common, which is about fifty acres of open land near the center of Boston's business district. It is the oldest public park in the United States. Not far from the park's gate is the monument honoring the Massachusetts 54th, the African-American Civil War Regiment from Massachusetts.

The next stop on the Freedom Trail is the State House, completed in 1798. Boston architect Charles Bulfinch designed the building. It has tall columns in front and a large round dome on top covered with copper. Inside hangs the state's "Sacred Cod." This wooden fish is carved out of a solid piece of pine. It represents the importance of the fishing industry in Massachusetts' history.

Many Italian stores and restaurants are in the North End.

Faneuil Hall marketplace was once a meeting place.

After that, you will pass the Park Street Church, the Granary Burying Ground, Kings Chapel and the Kings Chapel Burying Grounds. These are the praying and resting places of some of Boston's early patriots, including Samuel Adams, Paul Revere, and John Hancock.

Plan to drop by Old South Meeting House where angry colonists met to plan the Boston Tea Party. Faneuil Hall and Quincy Market are next.

The USS *Constitution* was the United States' first warship. Today it is located at the Charlestown Navy Yard, where you can take a tour of the ship.

Before the American Revolution, Boston patriots met at Faneuil Hall to discuss their plans. Now this area offers dozens of shops and restaurants. There's even a store for magic tricks and one for gems and fossils.

As you continue on the Freedom Trail, you will come to the world's oldest fully commissioned warship. It is the USS Constitution, also called "Old Ironsides." Free tours allow you to visit onboard the ship. More than 3,000 original artifacts from the ship are on display in a nearby museum.

There are many more wonderful sights in Boston. The Children's Museum is just for kids! It has many programs where you can take charge of the action. You can see yourself on TV in "Arthur's World." Or you can try out a storm rescue by putting on storm clothes and stepping into a life-sized boat. The Museum of Science offers an observatory where you can learn about the sky and stars. If you like dinosaurs, stop in at the Harvard Museum of Natural History.

Be sure to visit the New England Aquarium. This aquarium has a giant ocean tank that is four stories high. It gives you a life-sized under-water view of sharks, giant sea turtles, and tropical fish. Save some time for a sea lion circus-style performance at the Aquarium.

If you like land animals, try an afternoon at the Franklin Park Zoo. They have a Butterfly Landing Zone, a Giraffe Savannah (plain), and an area where you can meet farm animals, hand to paw.

No trip to Boston would be complete without a ride on its subway, the MBTA. You might also enjoy crossing the Charles River into Cambridge, the home of Harvard University and the Massachusetts

Institute of Technology (MIT). If you cross the Charles River on the "T", as residents call the Boston subway, stop at Kendall Square to see MIT. Hop back on to ride to Harvard Square where you will find singers, mimes, jugglers, magicians, and even actors performing free on the street corners. Put a donation in the hat if you like the performance.

These street musicians are entertaining at Harvard Square in Cambridge.

CHAPTER FIVE

THE PEOPLE AND PLACES OF MASSACHUSETTS

The people of Massachusetts are as different as its land. It is a state that is small in land size but large in the number of people who live there. More than six million people live in Massachusetts.

About eight out of every ten Bay Staters live in cities or towns. More than half of the state's city dwellers, about 600,000, live in Boston. Boston is the largest city in the state and its capital. Other large Massachusetts cities include Worcester, Springfield, Lowell, Cambridge, Brockton, and New Bedford. The state's smallest town is Gosnold. Fewer than 100 people live there.

People enjoy rafting on the Deerfield River.

THE PEOPLE OF MASSACHUSETTS

Many different groups enrich Massachusetts. According to the most recent figures, about eight out of every ten people in Massachusetts were born in the United States. Their heritage is mainly Irish, English, Italian, French, Portuguese, and Polish. If you put one hundred Bay State residents in a room, on average, five would be African-American, four or five would be Hispanic, two would be Asian, and there would be one Native American.

Throughout the year, Bay Staters share the food, games, dances, and

These pastries look delicious in an Armenian bakery in Watertown.

music of their cultures at the state's many ethnic festivals. January and February bring celebrations of Chinese and Japanese New Year, complete with parades that include dragons and firecrackers. Boston's Irish are famous for their St. Patrick's Day parade in March. Every summer, Boston's Italians hold weekend festivals in the North End. Stop by for some "gelato," an Italian ice cream, or try a cool refreshing Italian lemon ice.

Summer is also the time of the Dragon Boat festival for Asian-Americans, Caribbean carnivals for Haitians, and a Puerto Rican festival. In the fall Germans share the fun of Octoberfest, and all nationalities celebrate during Boston's International Festival in November.

WORKING IN MASSACHUSETTS

There are many different jobs available in Massachusetts. The state is number six in the country in manufacturing—making things for people to buy. Eleven out of every hundred people in the state work in manufacturing. Sixteen of America's biggest companies, like Gillette and Polaroid, have their headquarters in Massachusetts. But they are no longer making shoes and textiles. Today, most of Massachusetts' factories make parts for computers, print and publish books and magazines, and make parts for machines and for equipment used in transportation.

Many people work in the service industry, which includes businesses such as hotels, health care, or restaurants. Thirty-five out of every hundred people work at jobs that provide services rather than make a product.

Many important industries in the state depend on scientific research.

The two most important services are tourism and finance (jobs that deal with money). Eleven out of every hundred people work in the financial industry. Boston is often called the financial capital of New England. It is also one of the nation's top three healthcare centers.

Farming, mining, and fishing are still important in the state. Marble and granite are mined here. The Washington monument in Washington, D.C. is made from Quincy granite.

Small farms are scattered all over the state, particularly in the central and western parts. If all the farmland were added up, the total would be only a bit more than one-tenth of the state's land. The top four farm products are nursery plants, cranberries (the largest production in the world), dairy farm products, and apples.

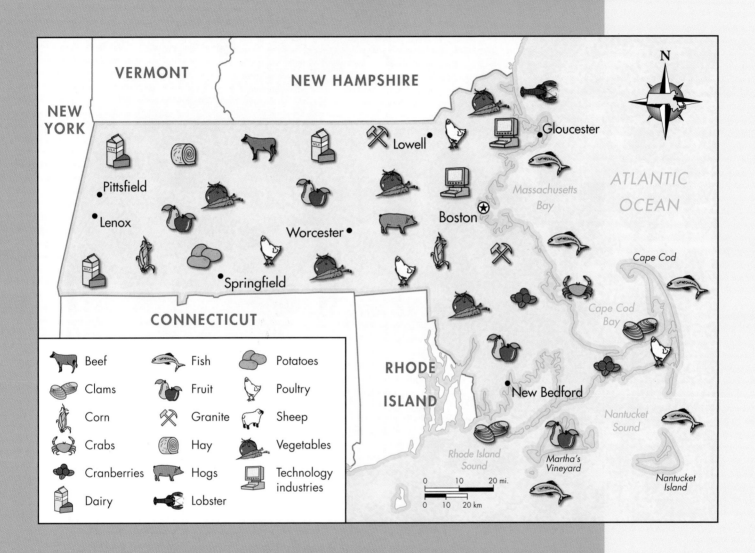

VERMONT

NEW HAMPSHIRE

NEW YORK

N

• Pittsfield

• Lowell

• Gloucester

ATLANTIC OCEAN

• Lenox

Boston ★

Massachusetts Bay

Worcester •

• Springfield

Cape Cod

Cape Cod Bay

CONNECTICUT

RHODE ISLAND

• New Bedford

Nantucket Sound

Rhode Island Sound

Martha's Vineyard

Nantucket Island

Beef	Fish	Potatoes
Clams	Fruit	Poultry
Corn	Granite	Sheep
Crabs	Hay	Vegetables
Cranberries	Hogs	Technology industries
Dairy	Lobster	

0   10   20 mi.

0   10   20 km

This crab fisher checks his catch.

The fishing industry's top three catches are cod, scallops, and flounder. New Bedford fishing crews bring in one half of the scallops caught in the entire United States.

SPORTS TEAMS

The people of Massachusetts are great sports fans. The Basketball Hall of Fame is in Springfield and the Volleyball Hall of Fame is in Mount Holyoke. The state's professional sports teams are located in Boston. The baseball team is the Boston Red Sox. Fenway Park, where the Red Sox play, is the oldest stadium in professional baseball. Hockey fans cheer for the Boston Bruins. Basketball fans follow the award-winning Boston Celtics. Fleet Center is home to the hockey and

Fenway Park is Boston's oldest professional baseball diamond. It opened in 1912.

EXTRA! EXTRA!

Many Bay Staters have contributed to sports. Frederick Winthrop Thayer was the captain of the Harvard Baseball Club when he received a patent for his baseball catcher's mask in 1878. The A.G. Spalding & Brothers Company in Chicopee invented the first basketball in 1894. William G. Morgan from Holyoke invented volleyball in 1895.

61

Chocolate chip cookies have been around since 1930—and they were first made in Massachusetts! A new tradition was born when Ruth Wakefield of Whitman first dropped chocolate into plain butter cookies. Remember to ask an adult for help!

CHOCOLATE CHIP COOKIES

1/2 cup butter
1/4 cup white sugar
1/2 cup brown sugar
1 tsp. vanilla
1 and 1/4 cup flour
1/2 tsp. baking soda
1/2 tsp. salt
1 egg
1 cup semisweet chocolate chips
1/2 cup chopped nuts (optional)

1. Preheat oven to 350°F.
2. Mix butter and sugars together in a bowl until blended.
3. Add egg and vanilla.
4. Mix dry ingredients together in a separate bowl.
5. Add to butter and sugar mixture.
6. Add the chips and nuts.
7. Stir together.
8. Drop the mixture by teaspoonfuls onto ungreased cookie sheets.
9. Bake the cookies one pan at a time, about eight minutes each.
10. When you take the hot cookie sheets out of the oven, use mitts to protect your hands.
11. Let the cookies cool for one minute on the sheet.
12. Remove cookies with a spatula and let them finish cooling on a cooling rack.

basketball teams. The New England Patriots and New England Revolution are the state's football and soccer teams. They both play in Foxboro Stadium.

TAKE A TOUR OF MASSACHUSETTS

All over the state, museums and living history parks allow visitors to peek at and even "experience" the past. Parks, beaches, mountains, and recreation facilities provide wonderful ways to enjoy the state. Shopping malls and factory stores, plays, concerts, and restaurants are ways to see, hear, and even taste the excitement that Massachusetts offers today.

Start your tour at the very tip of Cape Cod in Provincetown. The dunes rise high above the road on the way into town. Portuguese restaurants and art galleries, artists at work and people returning from a day of

The Head of the Meadows Beach on Cape Cod is a national seashore.

63

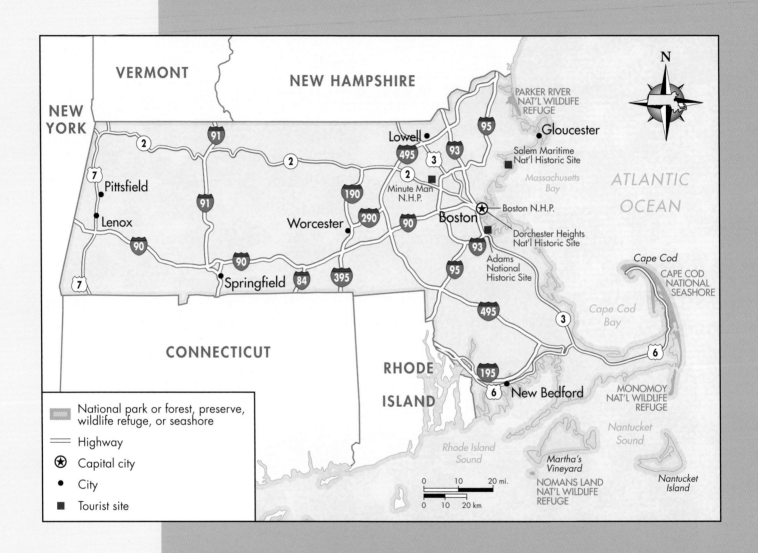

National park or forest, preserve, wildlife refuge, or seashore

Highway

Capital city

City

Tourist site

whale watching share the streets in this beautiful place. Then drive down to Wellfleet and stand where Guglielmo Marconi, an Italian scientist who lived in the United States, sent the first radio message across the ocean.

Farther down the highway are the beaches and shops of Hyannis, where President John F. Kennedy and his family spent summer vacations. If you like potato chips, you might want to visit the Cape Cod Potato Chip Factory. In Sandwich visit the home of Thornton Burgess, the creator of Peter Rabbit and other animal characters.

Before you leave the Cape, try some lobster and munch on a clam roll or a fried clam sandwich. Delicious! Hunt seashells on the beach and take the ferry to one or both of the state's large islands—Nantucket and Martha's Vineyard. The Vineyard is about nine miles wide and twenty-three miles long. In the summer, about 100,000 people crowd onto the island. Oysters and blue-shell crabs caught in local ponds are served in clam chowder in all the restaurants. Nantucket is three miles

Martha's Vineyard has many charming villages.

wide and about fifteen miles long. It's a little less crowded than Martha's Vineyard. Sample Nantucket Bay scallops and homemade Portuguese bread.

South of Boston, be sure to visit Plimoth Plantation. This is a living museum where costumed interpreters play the part of real Pilgrims. They explain what life was like for the Pilgrims in 1647 and you can see them at work. Climb onboard a replica of the *Mayflower* and see a Native American village—the home of Hobbamock, another Native American friend of the Pilgrims.

Nearby Cranberry World is a wonderful place to learn more about these berries, native to the state of Massachusetts. More than half of all the cranberry juice sold in the United States comes from Massachusetts.

Gloucester and New Bedford are also worth visiting. New Bedford has a very exciting National Historic Park devoted to whaling. You can learn what life was like on a whaling ship and take a tour of the many stops on the New Bedford Underground Railroad.

While in Quincy, be sure to stop at Adams National Historical Park and visit the farm that belonged to President John Adams and his son, President John Quincy Adams. Lexington and Concord, where the first shots were fired in the Revolutionary War, are just a few miles outside Boston. You can visit Minute Man National Historical Park. In Concord you can tour the homes of some of Massachu-

These boats sit in the port at Gloucester.

The Naismith Basketball Hall of Fame is in Springfield.

opposite:
A hiker looks out over the Berkshires.

setts' most famous authors—Louisa May Alcott, Ralph Waldo Emerson, and Nathaniel Hawthorne.

Salem is also north of Boston. There is a museum devoted to the witchcraft trials. However, several tours emphasize Salem's importance as a shipping port.

In Central Massachusetts, Old Sturbridge Village offers living history so you can experience life in the 1830s. Leominster is the birthplace of the state's folk hero, Johnny Appleseed.

The western part of the state draws music lovers in the summer and skiers in the winter. Spring and autumn bring beautiful flowers and colorful trees. Tanglewood Music Festival is held from June through early September in Lenox. The town is considered a fine summer resort. There are miles of hiking trails and a wildlife sanctuary nearby. Western Massachusetts is home to the Pratt Museum in Amherst and the Science Museum in Springfield. Each museum has displays of dinosaur bones and fossils. Springfield is also home to a firearms museum and the Naismith Basketball Hall of Fame. In Deerfield you can watch candlemaking at the Yankee Candle Factory.

Stockbridge, on the western edge of the state, was home for twenty-five years to artist Norman Rockwell. He painted many pictures that were used for magazine covers—many of them were of children.

One of the state's newest museums, the Massachusetts Museum of Contemporary Art, is in North Adams. This museum has twenty-seven buildings. It does not just display art, it shows large pieces of art that don't fit in other museums and often combines a display of art with performance!

The Mohawk Trail (State Route 2) is not to be missed. This road is best seen in fall when the leaves are changing colors. The trail is a road that was an Indian path and later became a road for wagons and now cars. Traveling it takes you back in time through a collection of small towns. Just off the trail are Mount Greylock, a natural bridge, and several wildlife sanctuaries. Shelbourne Falls and North Adams are the major towns on the route.

MASSACHUSETTS ALMANAC

Statehood date and number: February 6, 1788; the 6th state

State seal: adopted 1780, made official in 1885

State flag: adopted 1780; revised, 1971

Geographic center: Worcester 71° 45' W and 42° 15' N

Total area/rank: 9, 241 sq. mi. (23,934 sq. km)/45th

Coastline/rank: 979 sq. mi. (2,536 sq. km); 7th

Borders: New York, Vermont, New Hampshire, Connecticut, Rhode Island, and the Atlantic Ocean

Latitude and longitude: Between 40° 14' and 42° 53' N and 73° 30' and 70° 5' W

Highest/lowest elevation: Mount Greylock, 3,491 ft (1,064 m)/beach, sea level

Hottest/coldest temperatures: 107°F (42°C) at New Bedford and Chester on August 2, 1975/-35°F (−37°C) at Chester on January 12, 1981

Land area/rank: 7,838 sq. mi. (20,300 sq. km)/45th

Inland water area/rank: 424 sq. ml. (1,098 sq. km)/ 35th

Population/rank: 6,349,097 (2000 Census)/13th

Population of major cities (2000 Census):
Boston: 589,141;
Worcester: 172,648;
Springfield: 152,082;
Lowell: 105,167;
Cambridge: 101,355;
Brockton: 94,304;
New Bedford: 93,768;
Fall River: 91,938

Origin of state name: Native American word meaning "place near the great hill"

Capital: Boston, since 1630

Number of counties: 14

Major rivers/lakes: Connecticut, Merrimack, Hoosic, Housatonic, Charles, Mystic, Blackstone, and Neponset Rivers; Quabbin Reservoir, Wachusett Reservoir

Farm products: Nursery plants, cranberries, dairy products, and apples

Manufactured products: Electronic goods, computer parts

Mining products: Granite

Fishing products: Cod, flounder, scallops

Motto: Ense petit placidam sub libertate quietem. (By the sword we seek peace, but peace only under liberty.)

Nickname: Bay State

Tree: American Elm

Flower: Mayflower

Bird: Black-capped chickadee

Game bird: Wild turkey

Fish: Cod

Dog: Boston Terrier, first purebred dog in America 1869 (English Bulldog/English Terrier)

Cat: Tabby cat

Horse: Morgan

Marine mammal: Right whale

Beverage: Cranberry juice

Berry: Cranberry

Gem: Rhodonite

Bean: Navy bean

Muffin: Corn muffin

Dessert: Boston cream pie

Cookie: Chocolate chip

Insect: Ladybug

Folk hero: John Chapman (1775–1845), known as Johnny Appleseed

Heroine: Deborah Samson

Shell: New England Neptune

Mineral: Babingtonite

Rock: Roxbury conglomerate or "puddingstone"

Historical rock: Plymouth Rock

Song: "All Hail to Massachusetts"

Folk dance: Square dance

Poem: "The Blue Hills of Massachusetts" by Katherine E. Mullen

TIME**LINE**

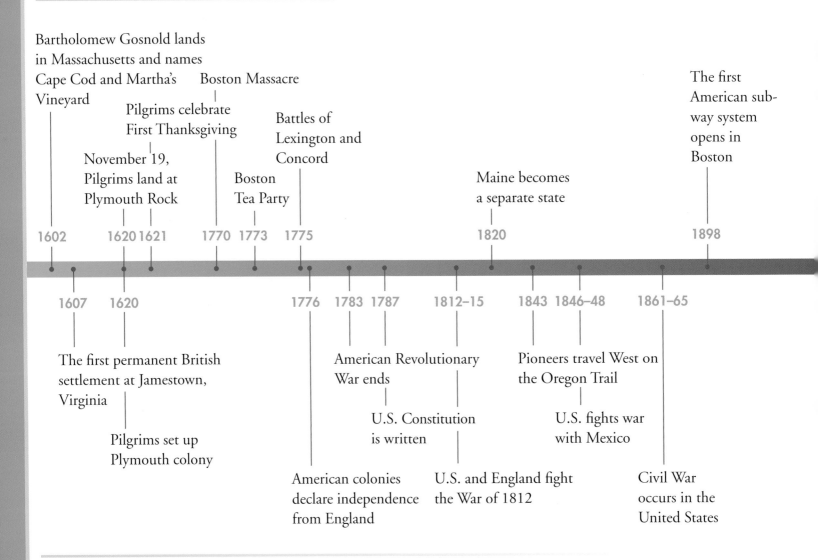

Bartholomew Gosnold lands in Massachusetts and names Cape Cod and Martha's Vineyard

Boston Massacre

The first American subway system opens in Boston

Pilgrims celebrate First Thanksgiving

Battles of Lexington and Concord

November 19, Pilgrims land at Plymouth Rock

Boston Tea Party

Maine becomes a separate state

1602   1620 1621   1770 1773   1775   1820   1898

1607   1620   1776   1783 1787   1812–15   1843   1846–48   1861–65

The first permanent British settlement at Jamestown, Virginia

American Revolutionary War ends

Pioneers travel West on the Oregon Trail

Pilgrims set up Plymouth colony

U.S. Constitution is written

U.S. fights war with Mexico

American colonies declare independence from England

U.S. and England fight the War of 1812

Civil War occurs in the United States

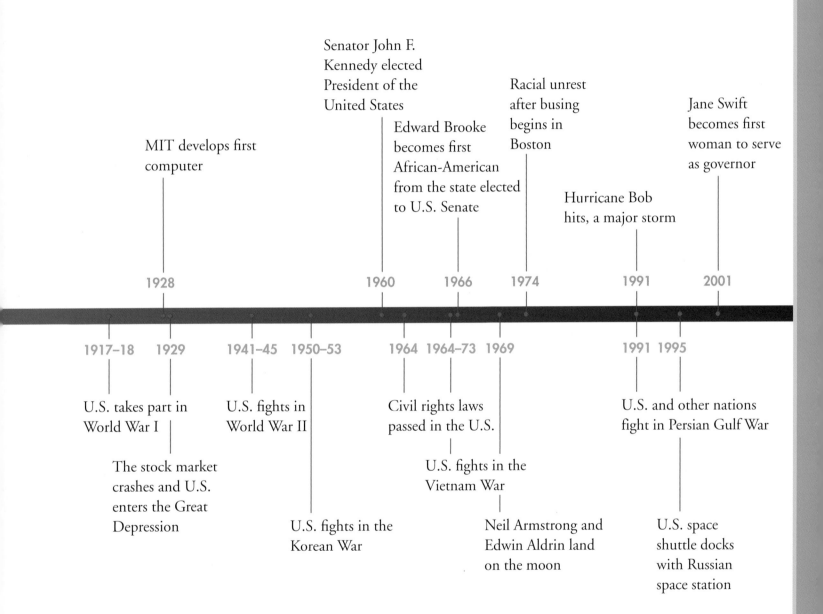

Senator John F. Kennedy elected President of the United States

Racial unrest after busing begins in Boston

Jane Swift becomes first woman to serve as governor

MIT develops first computer

Edward Brooke becomes first African-American from the state elected to U.S. Senate

Hurricane Bob hits, a major storm

1928

1960

1966

1974

1991

2001

1917–18   1929   1941–45   1950–53   1964   1964–73   1969   1991   1995

U.S. takes part in World War I

U.S. fights in World War II

Civil rights laws passed in the U.S.

U.S. and other nations fight in Persian Gulf War

The stock market crashes and U.S. enters the Great Depression

U.S. fights in the Vietnam War

U.S. fights in the Korean War

Neil Armstrong and Edwin Aldrin land on the moon

U.S. space shuttle docks with Russian space station

GALLERY OF FAMOUS BAY STATERS

Susan B. Anthony
(1820–1906)
Fought to improve the rights of women, especially the right to vote. Born in Adams.

Leonard Bernstein
(1918–1990)
Well-known symphony orchestra conductor and composer. Born in Lawrence.

Rachel Fuller Brown
(1898–1980)
Scientist. Helped to develop a drug that kills fungus infections of the skin and digestive system. Born in Springfield.

George Bush
(1924–)
Forty-first President of the United States. Born in Milton.

Thornton W. Burgess
(1874–1965)
Creator of popular animal characters Peter Rabbit and friends. Born in Sandwich.

Emily Dickinson
(1830–1886)
Poet. Lived in Amherst.

Robert Goddard
(1882–1945)
Called the "Father of Space" because his research on rockets laid the foundation for the U.S. space program. Born in Worcester.

Theodor Geisel (Dr. Seuss)
(1904–1991)
Children's author of *The 500 Hats of Bartholomew Cubbins, And To Think That I Saw It on Mulberry Street, The Sneetches, The Cat in the Hat,* and more. Born in Springfield.

Percival Lowell
(1855–1916)
Astronomer who built the Lowell Observatory in Flagstaff, Arizona to study the planet Mars. In 1930 Pluto was discovered by astronomers at the Lowell Observatory. Born in Boston.

John Fitzgerald Kennedy
(1917–1963)
Thirty-fifth president of the United States. He was the first Roman Catholic president. Born in Brookline.

GLOSSARY

abolish: to put an end to or get rid of something

amendment: a change made to improve or correct something

assassinate: to kill an important person

mandatory: something that has to be done

militia: a group of citizens who receive military training but who are called into action only in emergencies

observatory: a place designed for watching the stars, planets, and/or weather

precipitation: water that falls to earth as rain, snow, sleet, or hail

protest: to complain or object

revolution: a complete change in government or rule

strike: to stop work (by employees) to gain better working conditions

subway: an underground train in a city

suffrage: the right to vote

FOR MORE INFORMATION

Web sites

Commonwealth of Massachusetts
http://www.state.ma.us/
A variety of information from state agencies.

Massachusetts Office of Travel and Tourism
http://www. mass-vacation.com
Information on things to do and places to see in Massachusetts.

Massachusetts Visitor Information Network
http://www. massvisit.net
Visitor information for all regions of Massachusetts.

Books

Biel, Timothy L. *Life in the North During the Civil War.* San Diego, CA: Lucent Books, 1997.

Hinman, Bonnie. *John F. Kennedy Jr.* Chelsea House-Pub., 2001.

Penner, Lucille Recht. *Eating the Plates: A Pilgrim Book of Food and Manners.* New York, NY: Aladdin Paperbacks, 1997.

Sewall, Marcia *People of the Breaking Day.* New York, NY: Aladdin, 1997.

Stein, R. Conrad. *The Boston Tea Party.* Danbury, CT: Children's Press, 1998.

Addresses

Massachusetts Office of Travel and Tourism
10 Park Plaza, Suite 4510, 13th Floor
Boston, MA 02116

Governor's Office
State House
Office of the Governor
Room 360
Boston, MA 02133

INDEX

ABOUT THE AUTHOR

Joan Leotta was born in Pittsburgh, Pennsylvania and, as a child, often vacationed on Cape Cod. She has been writing since she learned how to read. Joan lives in Burke, Virginia with her husband, Joe, children Jennie and Joe, a lot of books, and a large seashell collection, including many from Cape Cod.

Joan says, "Reading and writing are partners. You can't do one without the other. Writing gives me a chance to explore many new ideas. I usually am able to include only about one-tenth of my research in my writings."

Photographs: A. Blake Gardner: 7, 9; AllSport USA/Matthew Stockman: 61; Bill Miles: 58; Corbis Sygma/Ira Wyman: 41; Corbis-Bettmann: 35; H. Armstrong Roberts, Inc.: 17 (J. Blank), 52 (R. Krubner), 3 left, 67 (J. Urwiller); Kindra Clineff: 4, 42, 50, 51, 54, 55, 56, 63, 65, 68, 69; Landslides Aerial Photography/Alex S. MacLean: 14; Library of Congress: 21; MapQuest.com, Inc.: 70; Monkmeyer/Arlene Collins: 60; North Wind Picture Archives: 31 left, 32, 33, 34; Photo Researchers, NY: 71 right (Tom Branch), 36 (Mark Marten/US National Library of Medicine), 71 left (James Zipp); Stock Boston/Leonard Harris: 18; Stock Montage, Inc.: 3 right, 22, 24, 25, 27, 28, 30, 31 right, 74 right, 74 top left, 74 bottom left; Stone: cover (Vito Palmisano), 48 (Chuck Pefley); Visuals Unlimited: 43, 46 (S. Berner), 11 (Steve Callahan).